The Heart of Sales

Success Secrets That Will Make You
Fall In Love With Sales

The Heart of Sales

J. D. Auguste

with R. Deon Butler

There is a fascinating correlation between the love and sales. *The Heart of Sales* makes learning sales simple and relatable.

These are the skills you need to succeed and the stories that make it worthwhile.

Editor: Horace Hord
ISBN: 0999308106
ISBN: 978-0-9993081-0-3
ISBN: 978-0-9993081-1-0
Printed in the United States of America

Preface

"There is purpose in the pain" sometimes can be the most annoying thing to hear when you are in the middle of your darkest days. This is especially so in those moments in life when you finally have no more answers and have also resolved in your spirit to ask no more questions and are drained from carrying the load of burdens too big for your shoulders, while the corners of your eyes sting from irritation because you've wiped countless tears. We've all experienced these seasons of heartache at various times throughout our lives.

When you are exhausted, angry, frustrated, and deliriously bitter with the entire world, even the mail carrier can become a villain in this horror story, delivering bills that you don't have the money to pay for. Right there in the middle of madness, as your thoughts bounce from wall to wall like echoes in an empty cave comes a friend who has the audacity to say, "There is purpose in the pain." As infuriating as that was for me to hear in that moment of space and time, that is exactly where the story of The Heart of Sales heard its very first heartbeats.

"Mom, this is not Haiti!" I said in a frustrated and almost disrespectful tone. My mother is a strong and resourceful woman, born on one of the most impoverished islands in the Caribbean. Survival was like a second language in the small island of Haiti. Mom wasn't fooled by my defensive confidence; she knew that my survival skills had their limits, and that limit was my pride.

My water had been turned off a couple of weeks at this point, and I had resorted to buying gallons of water from the grocery store to bathe. During one of her visits to my place in Fort Myers, Florida, my mother reminded me that although my water had been turned off, I could still flush the toilets by pouring water directly into the bowl.

Trying to appear strong, I smirked at her and said, "I know, Mom; that's what I've been doing."

Then she looked over her right shoulder, gazing out of my patio's glass doors at the lake behind my house and said something that provoked my "This is *not* Haiti" outburst. "If you run out of money and need to reserve your gallon water for bathing, just go out to the lake and fetch some water to care for the bathrooms."

"Lady, are you crazy," I thought to myself, not stupid or brave enough to say it aloud.

Even though she meant well, I was offended that Mom would recommend such drastic measures. How embarrassing would that be? I would *never* walk to the lake with a pail, with my neighbors possibly watching through their patios as I fetched water out of the lake to bring inside my house to flush the toilets! Her advice only made me more upset that I was in a financial bind that would warrant such primitive methods to even be an option. Didn't she know who I was?

I held a respected sales trainer position with one of the nation's largest telecom providers, a Fortune 50 company, and I had my own office at work. I lived in a beautiful gated community, in a cozy two-story town house with a garage and a stunning lake view. Every day I dressed liked the lost *GQ* model of South Florida, because I loved clothes, and my dad always taught me to be conscious of my appearance. On the outside, I appeared to have it all together, but internally I was struggling to get a handle on things, and it was like trying to hold water, literally.

About a week later, I was tiptoeing out to the lake with a pale in one hand and a fishing rod in the other. The fishing rod was to fool any of my neighbors who may have been witnessing this most humbling moment in my life. My water being turned off was only a fraction of my problems.

Life's challenges were in full swing. I may have had no water, but I was drowning in the floods of chaos that surrounded me. It was during those difficult times in my life that my friend and colleague R. Deon Butler would say, "There is purpose in the pain."

Then one night, in the silence of the hour, while I was kneeling down in prayer in the middle of my living room, this vision of *The Heart of Sales* dropped into my spirit. I had no water and by this time no electricity either, but on this night, I had life!

So, I extend to those who are reading this book and currently experiencing the difficulties of life while trying to pursue their dreams that "there is purpose in the pain!" What you may be feeling are birthing pains, and any mother will testify that although the birthing process can be extremely painful, she pushes through the pain because of purpose. May the desire to hear the heartbeat of your dreams also push you forward.

Acknowledgments

My son, Josiah, for everything I could not find the strength to do for myself, I found that strength when I thought about you. Your bright spirit and sense of humor kept me standing through some of life's most difficult challenges. I noticed how brilliant you were from a very young age, and I wanted to do everything I could to get you all that you needed in life; this is for you.

My brothers Jean and Steve, we have come a long way since the days we played paper airplane in the family room or *Doom* in the garage, rolling around in a carton tube. If there is one thing we learned during those times, it is that you start with what you have and use the power of your imagination to create a world of your own. I encourage you both to maximize all that God has put on the inside of you. The only thing holding the lion within us down is us.

My beautiful sisters, Esther and Rachel, you were born in the same month, but you are both very different and unique. Rachel, thank you for always calling me to check up on me. Sometimes my days were lonely. However, you always made sure you called to show you cared. I admire your strength, focus, and drive. Esther, I thank you for your free-spirited nature. Our conversations were always a joy, and what I learned from you may be just as much as you learned from me. Maybe not. Your spirit is one of pure gold; never forget that.

Dad, I appreciate all that you have taught us by your words and by your deeds. You've instilled work ethic, integrity, discipline, and strength in my life. You have not been perfect, and neither have I, yet even in your imperfection, you taught me about the grace and favor of God.

My brother, Rashaun Butler, road dog, business partner, and best friend, I praise God for you constantly. Men of great character and loyalty help to impact the lives of those who are in their realm of influence. Your friendship has seen me through a lot, and I am honored that we get to take this journey together. Thank you for the insight, feedback, and the creative flair that you invested into this book. Continue to grow into the man God called to fulfill His will.

Last, but not least, Mom. The world may never know how beautiful a spirit and how powerful a woman you are, but your children know. Your endurance amazes me, and when nothing seemed to be going right, you remained strong. Thank you for your prayers, your encouragement, the food, your wisdom, and your patience. When they ask me how I got to where I am, I will have to be honest and say, "Because of my God and my momma!" I love you, Mon Cheri.

Contents

Foreword

When J.D. and I first met, I was a new direct-sales rep who had never sold door to door, and he was already established as one of the top sales reps in our department. I noticed that most of the sales reps kept to themselves, and there was not much of a team culture, nor was there much of a structure for onboarding new hires, which resulted in a lack of training.

Although J.D. was not a part of the minimal class training I did receive, and he was not the sales rep who I was sent to shadow in the field, he asked me early on how I was doing and showed interest in my background and my career path. We established a friendship from that moment and began to share best practices when we had success, and during sales droughts, we would often encourage each other. I feel that J.D. was an integral part of the success that I had on our direct-sales team as I ascended to win top-seller awards, receive recognition, and, ultimately, gain my promotion into management and begin leading my own direct-sales team.

I believe that this book is an essential tool for any aspiring salesperson or any active salesperson who is looking to increase his or her sales volumes, prospecting, and overall customer/client relationships and networks. In my seven years as a sales leader, I have seen firsthand the many pitfalls that can easily be a snare to sales professionals, and J.D.'s book will help these individuals achieve the highest probability of success.

I have hired hundreds of sales reps for three different departments, and fewer than two dozen lasted longer than a year before being fired for poor performance or resigning to avoid that inevitability. During my time as a sales leader, I recognized the importance of ongoing sales training for my teams. This book will help ordinary people sell like professionals. You will learn how to prospect efficiently, create an efficient sales process, get commitments before the close, find the value of what the customer needs are, avoid wasting time with low-probability prospects, deliver a better sales presentation, and overcome objections before you even hear them.

J.D. has more than ten years of sales experience, and I was able to observe firsthand some of the key attributes he possesses that make him a fantastic sales leader and trainer. J.D. knows how to prepare multiple sales processes. Whether it is door to door or increasing sales for small-business owners, he has helped others to do so, and his success validates his teachings.

J.D. has a unique and natural ability to build a rapport that establishes trust from the beginning and sustains longer-term relationships after the close, which brings referrals. More importantly, it is his ability to teach others to perform in like manner. J.D. is a motivational speaker who has won awards for his efforts assisting others to maximize their sales potential.

After I had become a direct-sales leader, the first person I asked to help train my new hires and failing reps was J.D. The results were evident, as my team went from the last place to first in less than six months! I owe a lot of that success to J.D.'s willingness to help train my team and the tools that he gave them to add to their sales processes and skill sets. It was during our time as teammates and coworkers that J.D. and I talked about the lack of training our company and department provided for such a challenging role and sales position.

J.D. expressed the desire to become a sales trainer within the company as he had been in his previous company. He did just that and became one of the top sales trainers in the company, often given special assignments that required his ability to help design new and improved class curriculum.

Whenever I was in need of assistance to train my team, it was no wonder why J.D. was the first person I called to help in my efforts to improve my team's sales numbers.

Readers of this book will find personal stories and great analogies that make sales simple to understand and practice, motivation to increase their drive, and advanced sales techniques. I believe this will transform the lives of those who take the time to read, reflect, and apply it to their sales careers.

Paxton Boyd, PA
Sales Manager and Realtor

Introduction

Consumers and salespeople alike have far too often misunderstood sales. Consumers have become increasingly skeptical of the true intentions of salespeople, and professionals have begun to associate the request to sell as pressurized stress. How has a skill set that should be appreciated and pursued become the villain in the minds of so many?

So I began to ask myself, "What went wrong and how can we fix it?"

The Heart of Sales takes a unique but relatable approach to teaching sales skills by looking at the sales process from the perspective of a relationship. Whether it is a potential mate, friend, or family member, relationships have been a part of our lives since the day we were born. We need them, learn from them, are frustrated by them, and are fulfilled by them.

Oddly enough, our relationship with sales has similar twists and turns to that of a dating relationship. Everything from the various stages of dating to everyday happenings can be associated with the sales process. In essence, by understanding these principles and their impact, we can improve both our ability to maximize sales and have more fulfilling relationships.

This is not just about how to sell but how to enjoy sales. When people enjoy what they do, they can reach new levels of success they never imagined reaching.

The techniques we discuss have been proven effective by thousands of new and veteran sales associates we've instructed during our time as sales trainers and from years of practical application. The real-life stories that are shared and the difficult lessons I learned from them are from my own experiences to help readers see the impact these techniques have had on my long-standing career in sales.

Sales skills are a vital element in the success of every business. We teach transferable skills applied in every type of sales channel, from direct face-to-face sales to over-the-phone sales transactions. This book speaks to a broad range of industry professionals, such as from real estate, insurance, car sales, multilevel marketing, small-business owners, and anyone who engages in the selling of products and services. Whether this is your first time learning sales or you are a seasoned veteran, this book will help you enjoy, teach, and learn the heart of sales.

It was like love at first sight. Let me stop lying; it was more like "let's make love the first night" in my mind, but I'm trying to ignore the temptations that's at the door facing my line of sight.

See, I heard that she was an around-the-way type, chasing dreams and whatever else that came down the pike. With multiple streams, some would say even multiple schemes, you see, she would try to excite most people by what she had in those jeans.

It seemed as if I was the only one that could read what her body screamed from across the room, and as soon as she walked in that green dress, her body talked to me; it was as if I was in a dream that had suddenly come true.

I mean, after all of the stress and the things that I have been through, understand I was ready to give this another try, but I had to reset my precepts in order to continue.

She grabbed a seat and a menu, looking at me as if I was the last one left in this venue. She smiled as I took a breath and began to reach out her hand, and as mine slowly followed suit, she opened her mouth as I began to stand and said, "Hi."

-The Heart of Sales

Chapter 1
Love At First Sight

Social Media QR Codes

A commonly debated theory in relationships is the notion of "love at first sight." Some people profess to have fallen in love with their significant other from the moment they first laid eyes on him or her, while others enjoy laughs over the challenges they experienced with their first encounters and how they could not have imagined hitting it off.

Whether you believe in love at first sight or a more progressive love, your perspective on love will affect the success

of your relationships. Likewise, in sales, your perspective will make or break you.

Align Your Perspective

"Perspective is defined as a particular attitude toward or way of regarding something; a point of view." Dictionary.com

The way you see sales will impact your effectiveness as a sales professional. It is the reason why two individuals can be in the same position yet experience two very different results: one making an unlimited amount of commission, but the other ready to pull out his or her hair from frustration. Perspective can sometimes be the difference between being married and being *happily* married.

Many people have trouble succeeding with sales because they have not properly learned the skill set, so they have an improper perspective of what sales is. When you do not have the right perspective of the selling opportunity, it becomes easier to lose sight of the goal you wish to accomplish. You will begin to focus your attention more on the obstacles instead of the opportunity.

Consider a car that has slowly begun to drift off track while driving; this happens as a result of the tires not being in perfect alignment. When your perspective does not align, your vehicle or "vocation" will gradually drift off track. The secret to unlocking uncapped income as a sales professional and increasing the productivity of your sales department resides in the six inches between your ears.

When cars do not function correctly, a tune-up will remedy the situation. A tune-up makes small changes to various parts of the vehicle, which improves the overall performance of the car. As you aim to build your sales mind-set and establish the right perspective for success, you will need to tune up your mechanics.

An automotive battery is a rechargeable battery that supplies electrical energy to a motor vehicle. It uses both a negative charge and positive charge to start the engine. Likewise, both negative and positive experiences are needed to have a rounded perspective of sales. A negative experience can be the best way to learn what *not* to do. Negative experiences do not justify a person having a negative perspective. There isn't a person alive who has not had negative relationship experiences, but the people who choose to use those experiences to learn eventually find themselves in the right relationship.

If the goal is to start the engine, a person must connect his or her positive and negative experiences to another energy source in order to jump-start the situation. This is why individuals or couples who seek relationship counseling experience new life and begin enjoying better relationships. Likewise, professionals who seek mentoring and other resources will continue to develop, despite their hardships.

Ask yourself, "What and who am I connected to?" Are they providing you a jump-start that will help you to learn from your positive and negative experiences? Are they pumping your mind with positive energy or are they simply draining your battery? Joel Osteen once said, "You're going to go through tough times—that's life. But I say, 'Nothing happens *to* you, it happens *for* you.' See the positive in negative events."

Developing a negative perspective can be a result of various experiences, but they break down into two sections: internal influence and external influence. Internal influences need to be tuned up, while external influences need to be tuned out. External influence comes from outside forces or people, while internal influence is created in your own mind based off your experiences. Understanding these two influences will help you to disconnect from energy-draining people and start on the road to living a more abundant life.

External Influences

When external forces guide your perspective of sales, you are more susceptible to the negative opinions others may have about sales. Effective salespeople are an asset to every business and create opportunities for a business to grow at a rapid rate. On the other hand, a negative and ineffective sales culture will hurt a business's chance of succeeding. If you don't learn how to tune out negativity, you will start to believe the adverse things other people may say about sales.

As I was going door to door one day as a direct-sales representative for Comcast, I came across a woman who initially opened her door but immediately slammed it shut in my face! As I walked down her driveway and passed by her mailbox, she swung open her door, came back outside, and yelled at the top of her lungs, "You should get a real job!" As I reflected on her statement, I realized that her perspective did not align with mine.

I was working for a Fortune 50 company and had a very flexible schedule; I was not micromanaged every second of the day and had nobody looking over my shoulder every minute of the day. I made upwards of $90,000 a year at the time, vacationed where I wanted and when I wanted, so I finally concluded that I did not want a "real" job by her definition! *You can't stop people from sending negativity to your mailbox, but that doesn't mean you have to open it.*

Many people who could thrive in a network marketing system sometimes give up too quickly simply because of external influences. If you believe in the product a company is selling and the structure that is in place is designed for others to prosper alongside you, then you cannot allow someone else's doubt or ignorance to make decisions for you. The life you seek to build is too important to place in the hands of other people.

I want to take a brief moment here to play heaven's advocate. There is a proverb that says, "In the multitude of counselors, there is safety" (Prov. 11:14). In other words, seeking advice from others is good and wise. I am sure that there are times in your life that you wished you listened to people who tried to warn you about someone or something. The goal here is not to tune out everyone.

The first thing we can learn from this proverb is that it says in the "multitude of counselors," meaning that you may need to implore a few trusted individuals to gain a more holistic perspective. Secondly, these counselors should be qualified to advise you. If you need guidance on a relationship decision, ask people who are in good relationships or who have foreseeable knowledge about relationships. If it is career-related guidance, speak to people who are successful in that field of study. Ultimately, the decision is yours to make, so consider all that you have learned and make a decision.

Internal Influence

Internal influence is the product of your own personal experiences with other people. In sales, your experiences as a customer are invaluable! They are opportunities to learn good practices that can attribute to your own sales success. However, when you allow your negative experiences to form your perspective, you will begin to believe that the ineffective practices of others are necessary for sales success.

For example, if you have interacted with salespeople who were pushy, dishonest, and manipulating, you may begin to feel that those are the traits of salespeople, causing you to become less attracted to becoming a salesperson. The truth is that you do not have to be any of those things. The misperception that you must be pushy to be a successful salesperson is a complete turn-off for most people. It turns what they may have seen as a great opportunity into an unattractive and sometimes unethical task.

The Heart of Sales is one of discipline, honesty, and character. People buy from people they like, so it is critical to use more of the skill set rather than a drill set when having a sales conversation. The "art of sales" is the ability to communicate the benefits of your product in an appealing manner to your customers. Business owners who are unskilled in the art of sales push their sales force to meet metrics without properly training them, thereby making a highly stressful work environment that can create pushy salespeople.

Use the methods discussed in this book, and you will never feel the need to be pushy ever again. Once you have the right skills, all you need to do is ensure that you are in the right market, know your product, and know that there is a need for your product. With a proper work ethic, which helps to ensure that you see enough people, you can create the ultimate sales environment that is fun to work in and gives the customer the freedom of choice to say, "Yes!"

Removing Doubt

The most beautiful thing you can wear is confidence.

—Blake Lively

Every man who has ever wanted to approach a beautiful woman has had to eliminate the voice of doubt in his head. Until he closes the curtains on his doubts, his confidence cannot take center stage. Whether you are in face-to-face sales or over the phone, people can sense confidence. It is almost impossible to persuade someone to believe in something or someone you do not believe in yourself.

Confidence is the state of being certain about something. Since there are many uncertainties in life and business, doubt can easily creep in and disable us from moving forward. To remove doubt, you must build confidence by becoming more certain. How? Simply learn more. The more you learn and know about your product, the more confident you will be when presenting it. The more you learn about your partner, the more certain you will be. The more you know about yourself, the more confident you will become.

Body Language

A study done by Professor Emeritus Albert Mehrabian, at UCLA, revealed that about 55 percent of communication is body language. Therefore, before you have said anything, you have already said everything. If a man walks into the door of his home and immediately sees his wife cut him with a razor-sharp stare, standing with her arms tightly crossed and vigorously tapping her feet, he knows something is wrong.

The wrong kind of body language can have a negative impact on a sales interaction, while positive body language can transfer confidence, which is important to make a positive impact. If you are face to face, keep your back straight, your shoulders back, and chin up. You want your feet to be aligned with your shoulders and your hands out of your pockets. When possible, turn to the side instead of face to face when showing the customer something. This process can help relax your customer because it is more common to see friends talking together.

Astonishingly, I believe people can hear your body language. Try saying, "I am so happy!" while displaying an angry face. Does it sound genuine? When selling over the phone, sit with your back straight or stand up instead of slouching. It is also a great practice to keep a mirror at your desk so that you can monitor your facial expression.

Hit the Reset Button

Your success as a sales professional has everything to do with your attitude. Most people will start a workday or workweek with a positive attitude, but the trick in sales is to maintain that position. Learning how to reset your attitude gives you power over your emotions. Attitude is when your way of thinking and feeling translate into your behavior. A negative attitude is extremely destructive for a sales professional because the customer can see the negative response even if the salesperson says all the right things.

Here is a list of negative feelings that destroy a sales transaction:

Frustration	Moodiness
Anger	Prejudice
Indifference	Aggravation
Sarcasm	Disconnectedness
Argumentativeness	Annoyance

These feelings do not usually appear after one bad interaction with a customer but creep in after numerous rejections. A salesperson can quickly begin to display these emotions without even knowing it. Hitting the reset button will prevent you from carrying negative energy and emotions from a prior interaction to a new opportunity. This way of thinking is what helps new relationships begin with a clean slate; however, many people fail to use this vital skill because of emotional baggage they carry for too long.

Meditate on this verse from the apostle Matthew 9:16 "No one sews a patch of unshrunk cloth on an old garment, for the patch will pull away from the garment, making the tear worse. Neither do people pour new wine into old wineskins. If they do, the skins will burst; the wine will run out, and the wineskins will be ruined. No, they pour new wine into new wineskins, and both are preserved." In essence, to preserve the new you, you cannot think like the old you.

If you begin a new relationship but fail to hit the reset button, you will probably penalize your new mate as a result of your old experiences. For this reason, taking the time to heal from a past relationship failure before engaging in a new one is recommended, or, sometimes, if more serious, counseling may be needed in order to help you to reset. Sales is no different. Although counseling would be a little dramatic for simply trying to get past a negative sales interaction, there are, however, creative methods to help you reset.

My former direct-sales manager told me about a method he used to reset his attitude after a bad interaction. As he reached the end of a person's driveway, he shook one leg as if he was dusting off his shoes. Customers who saw him would ask, "What are you doing?"

He replied, "I am shaking off the negativity and leaving it here."

It may sound a little silly, but it helped him reset his attitude and start fresh at the next door.

You could crumple up a paper ball to signify the last interaction and throw it away if you work indoors; just don't throw it at another employee. That'd turn into an HR issue. The method you use is not as important as the mind-set you wish to create, so the key is to reset your mindset in preparation for the next customer. So be creative!

Every sales opportunity is unique because every customer is unique. Even when you experience similar situations throughout your workday, you must remember that your next customer is not your previous customer. Your new relationship is not your previous failed relationship. Remember to hit the reset button so that you are approaching your new opportunities with new energy.

I recall specifically having a tough day one day as a residential sales rep, in which I had no sales and almost no time left before I had to go home. I was frustrated, tired, and, to be honest, tired of seeing no results. Feeling discouraged, I thought about giving up on the day and heading back to my car. The thought of going home with a doughnut—zero—was not appetizing, so I decided to hit the reset button one more time and knock on a few more doors.

As I walked across the street to the next house and made my way up the driveway, the family who lived at that home pulled up in their black SUV. Before I could even say my intro, the man driving the SUV saw the company I worked for and said, "I was just about to call you guys." He immediately invited me inside and asked me to sign him up for all our services. The gentleman even offered me a slice of cake that his daughter had made.

Aristotle once said, "It is the mark of an educated mind to be able to entertain a thought without accepting it." In my frustration, I entertained the thought of giving up on the day and going home, but I didn't accept it. Although I did accept the cake he offered me after the smell of sweet victory filled the air.

Needless to say, I walked away from that interaction with a sale, a freshly baked slice of cake, and a great example of the power of the reset button.

If you were to ask any IT professional what is the first thing that he or she would do when attempting to troubleshoot a computer-related issue, more often than not, you will find that the IT professional will first reset the PC before attempting any troubleshooting methods. I believe that there will be days the sales universe will test your ability to maintain your attitude. When you decide to hit the reset button, you can have your cake and eat it too!

Yeah, I must confess she had me at hello, or could it have been that green dress that hypnotized my mind as she approached, or maybe as I reflect, it could've been the design of the seams or the patterns that caught her eye on my clothes. But after she said "Hi," my reply was out of this world. I'm talking Saturn, the way she had my head in the sky, already wanting to put a ring around her globe, but I couldn't jump the broom just yet, though.

So after that cheesy line about being the best man, her hand is what I let go and sat down and listened as her plan began to unfold. She had grabbed my attention, but at first, my intention was to get a quick fix, not a pension, and move on to the next chick, though, I had to admit that this one felt kind of different.

So after we had talked for a minute, she

asked if I wanted to go on the floor—you know, cut a rug. I shoulder shrugged and told her that back in the day I was known to have broken a few Guinness—you know, records—but we can play. She said, "Okay, if that's how you would like to spin it."

This game that was being played I later found out was merely a scrimmage 'cause I went from talking to finding myself walking out of this place the same way I had entered...Alone.

-The Heart of Sales

Chapter 2
You Had Me at Hello

Social Media QR Codes

Long after you have left, people will remember you by the impression you made on them. Since a second chance is not guaranteed, both men and women normally do their best to make a good first impression on each other. Men wear their finest clothes and favorite cologne. A woman might put on her best dress and get her hair, nails, and eyebrows done to prepare for her first impression.

A young man meeting his girlfriend's parents for the first time will commonly be very mindful of his manners, making sure to say "sir" and "ma'am." If he is smart, he will bring his girlfriend some lovely flowers to make an even better impression. Making a good first impression increases the probability of building trust. While a bad impression is hard to shake, a good first impression is simply unforgettable!

Make an Impression

"Impression is defined as a characteristic, trait, or feature resulting from some influence." Dictionary.com

Icebreakers

Hopefully, you have moved past your days of using cheesy pickup lines. I am a little tempted to include an example in this paragraph for a little comic relief, but I won't do it. All right, I lied. "Do your feet hurt? Because you've been running through my mind all day long." Now that I have gotten that out of my system, we can move forward. Pickup lines are cheesy because they are in fact cheesy and typically ineffective, especially if someone is already not interested in giving you a chance. An icebreaker, on the other hand, could be the spontaneous, unexpected, and sincere comment you need to extend the conversation.

Making an initial connection can be tough because people tend to want to get rid of salespeople. Do not take it personally. Most people have a preconceived idea about salespeople, and your job is to help them understand your positive intentions by being engaging. Your personality is all you need to show someone that you are not like the last salesperson with whom he or she had a negative experience.

One way to overcome this is to use an icebreaker that will catch the customer off guard and lead the conversation in a direction the customer was not expecting.

Customers say no immediately because they feel like they know what you are going to say, and they have heard it all before. But if you say what they do not expect, it freezes them. If you are in a call center where you have to read a script, you can still do this and get right back to your script.

I am not referring to the basic "How's the weather?" or "How are you today?"—icebreakers that customers have learned to expect. A highly efficient icebreaker requires your real personality and your undivided attention. When done correctly, you will appear to be quick on your feet and witty, but there is more structure than most people realize.

Read, Relate, Relax

Read, Relate, Relax is a technique that can help you formulate an effective icebreaker.

Read your environment. Observe the environments of your customers, review their account, or listen for cues. Identify something that stands out to you that could be a good conversation starter. It could be something at the customer's home if you are in residential sales or something the client is wearing or holding if you are in an indoor environment. Even if you are over the phone, look at the overview of the customer's account, or listen for cues that can help you grab the customer's attention.

Relate it back to yourself. This process is where your personality takes center stage. Take whatever you have selected to use as an icebreaker and ask yourself, "What does it mean to me?" The more genuine your icebreaker is, the more efficient it will be. Sometimes the first thing that comes to mind is a compliment and that is fine, but there are other effective methods as well. Maybe what you notice, reminds you of a funny story or a particular experience in your life. Tell them! Maybe it prompts a question.

Ask them! You may be surprised when you are sincere how receptive people actually are.

Relax the situation. The goal is that your icebreaker will help the customers relax and stop them from giving you the immediate "No." If you spark a real conversation, let it flow for a little before jumping into your script or presentation.

SEE Principle

A useful technique that can also help improve your introduction is something known as the SEE principle. Below are the three elements of this principle.

Smile because smiling is contagious. Have you ever noticed that you naturally smile back at someone in the hallway or the grocery store, only because he or she smiled at you? It is a natural reaction to smile back. Especially if you are in a face-to-face sales environment, flashing a genuine Colgate smile can make a world of difference.

Eye Contact builds trust with your customer. A common mistake that salespeople make is not maintaining eye contact as they speak. This process does not mean that looking briefly away will cause a problem, but when introducing yourself or presenting information, eye contact helps customers feel your confidence and helps them to believe your message. It also helps you to focus on the interaction and avoid being distracted by things in the environment.

Enthusiasm rubs off on the customer. You cannot expect someone to be excited about something for which you display no excitement. Most people are skeptical of salespeople early in the interaction, but you can overcome skepticism by sustaining a natural level of enthusiasm. Your customer will become less worried about what you want and become more interested in why you are so excited.

Appearance

As the saying goes, "You don't get a second chance to make a first impression." If you have experienced a blind date, then you know how true this statement can be. This statement is also true in sales. As a sales professional, you realize that you do not have very long to make that first impression. Most salespeople will have only fifteen to thirty seconds to make a positive first impression on a potential customer, so it is important to understand which elements have the biggest impact.

The most prominent part of a first impression is your appearance. The way you look can tell a customer how seriously he or she should consider what you are presenting. It is true that a client can make an incorrect assessment about you if he or she tries to judge a book by its cover, but you can also send out the wrong message if you avoid this truth. The power of perception always lies firmly in your hands.

In face-to-face sales, appearance is even more critical. Not only your appearance but also the appearance of your marketing material makes a difference. What impression might you make potential customers if you hand them marketing material that got dirty in your car or badly wrinkled in your workbag? Remember, your overall appearance is a representation of your business and more importantly, your brand. Take time to iron your work clothes so that you do not look like a wrinkled sheet of paper. Wear clean shoes, practice good hygiene, and groom correctly.

When I was working door to door for Comcast, one of the nation's largest cable companies, there was a full-length mirror next to the exit door so that you could check your appearance before leaving the office. Over that mirror was a sign that read, "Would you buy from you?" I believe that is a good question to ask yourself before leaving your house every day.

Even if you are not engaging in face-to-face sales, your appearance can still affect your performance because appearance affects confidence. As a sales trainer, I was not surprised to see many of the top sales representatives dressed professionally in a call center. When you look good, you feel good, and I believe customers can hear it in your voice.

Another aspect of your appearance that a client notices over the phone is your facial expression. It is common for a company to provide its phone reps with a mirror to keep at their desks so that they can be aware of their facial expressions. The phrase "I can see it all over your face" speaks to the fact that our emotions manifest in our expressions, which eventually shows up in our voices.

Body Language

Human communication is 20 percent verbal and 80 percent nonverbal. New research by a pair of Stanford scientists also revealed that nonverbal cues can indicate a person's ability to learn and the strength of his or her creative skills. This research suggests that your body language not only affects what a customer learns from you but also what you can learn from him or her. We will discuss later how you can learn from a client's body language, but let us first consider how your body language helps you gather information.

Positive body language communicates to your brain that you are ready and focused on the task at hand and prepares you to notice the primary signals. Consider football players at the line of scrimmage and how they firmly hold their stance while surveying the players on the opposite team. Their body language tells their brains to focus on even the most subtle movements from their competition so that they can respond instantly.

The quarterback has to be even more in tune with the body language of the opposing defense. Peyton Manning, a future Hall of Fame quarterback, who played eighteen seasons in the National Football League (NFL) was a master at reading body language. His accomplishments were great and many during his time in the league, but he is profoundly remembered for his ability to call audibles. An 'audible' is when a quarterback sporadically changes the initial play call at the line of scrimmage because of something he sees in the defense.

Understanding that body language is communication, being aware of your body language should be a no-brainer. However, an advanced sales technique is knowing when and how to change your posture based off something you perceive from the customer. In other words, know when to call an audible. If my customer appears skeptical, I can turn to the side and show them my brochure. Changing my position so that we stand side by side, instead of face to face decreased the feeling of confrontation and made it feel like two friends talking.

The same applies to professional poker players who have to be mindful of their body language. For example, squared shoulders, high chin, and relaxed breathing will help a poker player control his or her body language. Being mindful of these behaviors will help prepare you to learn at the very beginning of the interaction.

Tone

Once you are more aware of your facial expressions and body language, you can begin to focus on your tone of voice. Managing your tone of voice is an essential skill because you convey various types of messages during a sales interaction. It is possible to lose a sale at any point in the conversation, all because you said something the wrong way. Establishing a proper tone of voice will help you connect better with your customer in the early stages.

One technique that can contribute to creating a relaxed atmosphere is to use a tone of voice your client may be familiar with or frequently hear. For example, if you are speaking to an elderly woman, you can try using a softer tone that may remind her of conversations with her grandchildren. Let us say you are speaking to a young professional; having a more assertive yet friendly tone might remind him or her of a coworker. The familiar sound can be more pleasing for the customer and help him or her to be comfortable when speaking with you.

Matching your tone with the client's personality works similarly. If the customer is reserved and friendly, you would be better received if you smile when speaking with him or her and sound relaxed. A customer with a friendly personality will appreciate the lightheartedness of that approach. It should feel like two friends having a conversation on a Saturday afternoon. Another customer who may be more direct and speak with a firmer tone of voice might appreciate a more formal conversation and tone of voice. No matter how you adjust your tone, your goal is to connect with customers on their level.

What You Say

The verbal aspect of confidence can be broken down to "What you say" and "How you say it." Some people say, "It does not matter what you say, but how you say it." I do not believe that to be entirely accurate. The language you use or "What you say" can give a customer confidence in your ability, trustworthiness, and experience.

Imagine taking your car to a mechanic who said that he or she has never worked on the model of your car before but would try it. How much confidence would you place in that person given that statement? Now imagine that another mechanic said to you that he or she has worked on cars similar to yours for over thirty years. Instantly there is a sense of relief that you may have the right person for the job.

Think about your skill sets, and identify those things that increase your ability to service your customer, whether it be your work experience, education, or knowledge of a particular subject. Communicate those things to help your customer have peace of mind about doing business with you. It is not bragging if it is true, so do not fret about coming across in a prideful way.

How You Say It

Improving "what you say" is easier because it only requires you to identify key points, make a note of them, and verbally communicate them. "How you say" something comes from a deeper place and may need more time to develop. Confidence is a belief, so the question you first have to ask yourself is, "Do I believe what I am saying?"

Honesty is a priceless virtue; however, it cannot help you sound more confident without proper application. All great speakers practice the art of public speaking because communication is a skill. Just like any skill, it takes work to improve. Toastmasters International is an organization that helps people to become more confident at speaking, and one of area of its focus is to decrease ineffective communication habits.

Confidence increases when you learn methods to decrease stuttering, mumbling, and use of verbal crutches, which help you sound more confident. Joining a group or taking a class that helps you improve your communication skills will pay in the end and make you feel more confident internally, which shows up externally.

Building Early Rapport

The income you earn in sales is a reflection of the relationships you build with customers. You have an opportunity with each experience to create a lasting memory with your customers, no matter how short the interaction. If you look at your customers as just another number, you will not reach your highest potential in sales. Relationships are the lifeblood of any business, and learning how to make meaningful connections is the heartbeat of sales success.

One method is most commonly used to find common ground with the customer. This method can be anything from kids, pets, sports, hobbies, music, and so on. The more diverse your ability to connect with different individuals, the more money you will make. The challenge sometimes is that you may not have anything in common with a particular customer, or the common ground that you do share is not that important to him or her.

One day as a door-to-door sales rep in South Florida, I walked up to a home, and before knocking on the door, I noticed that the homeowner was a Miami Heat basketball fan. I took note of the logo on the license plate and a Miami Heat flag in the window of the home. When the homeowner answered the door, my first words were about how I would not be able to assist him in saving money, seeing that he was rooting for the wrong team. The man took my lighthearted and sarcastic approach well and instantly began a friendly conversation about my mistake in not being a Miami Heat fan.

After talking for a few minutes about the current condition of my Chicago Bulls and their struggle to be relevant after the Michael Jordan era, the man went inside his home briefly to check with his wife about my offer. He returned with a yes and a bottle of water. My approach allowed us to build an instant rapport very early and contributed to the customer making a buying decision because he liked me.

Most people understand the importance of building rapport, but they can still be ineffective due to making an incorrect assumption or stereotyping a customer during their efforts to connect. This deficiency is usually a fatal blow to the sales transaction because the customer may feel insulted by the assumption. Be aware of stereotypes that form because of your previous interactions with a particular customer segment.

When we stereotype, we assume that everyone in a particular group has the same values and will behave similarly to others that fit that stereotype. For example, the stereotype that all senior citizens are slow and resistant to new technology can prove valid on numerous occasions, but accepting this stereotype as an absolute truth will cause a salesperson to miss many opportunities. If you are willing to learn, sales will teach you to appreciate other groups of individuals, cultures, and family systems.

I remember sitting in the car, thinking was I wrong for the way it had ended. See, I pretended that I wasn't offended by her tone when she said that she had some interest but hadn't committed to anyone in a minute, let alone in a second. See, I was expecting for her to give it to me 'cause I thought I had shown that I could handle my business and could meet whatever the objective; all I needed was just an entrance.

Apparently, that entrance soon turned into an exit, 'cause the instant I suggested if she would be 100 percent vested, it was like she was no longer convinced and felt the need to undress it. So now I'm on the fence 'cause I'm not understanding her methods.

"Were you looking for someone or not?" It's like we're in a group text, yet I'm the one that's perplexed on the other end, receiving the mixed message.

So much for the suspense, 'cause after leaving somewhat disrespected, my phone started to ring, and I'm questioning whether or not I need to accept it, but after the second ring, I leaned over to see where I left it and to my surprise on the screen what I see was a blessing.

-The Heart of Sales

Chapter 3
I Would Like to Get to Know You

Social Media QR Codes

In a love relationship, one of the most exhilarating yet frightening phases is when you are getting to know each other. This phase never actually ends, since humans tend to evolve and change over time, but the early interactions are critical to the longevity of the relationship. This is a stage in a relationship where the most important questions are asked to uncover a person's likes, dislikes, dreams, goals, aspirations, and family values. Asking the right kind of questions can mean the difference between

"Happily Ever After" and "I wish I never met you." It is no wonder that marriage counselors ask critical questions of a couple considering marriage when helping a couple uncover possible blind spots in their relationship.

Similarly, the discovery step in a sales conversation is vital to better understanding the endless possibilities in a particular situation. Questions allow a salesperson to identify blind spots that a customer may have never considered and set the foundation for establishing a lasting relationship.

Probe their globe

"Probing means to seek to uncover information about something or someone." Dictionary.com

Asking Questions

I never learn anything talking. I only learn things when I ask questions.

—Lou Holtz

I want you to imagine that you've met someone, and at some point you agree to go grab coffee with him or her. As you walk into the coffee shop, the aroma of roasted coffee beans stimulates your senses. The smooth mellow atmosphere accompanied by a slight bounce from the jazz music playing softly in the background sets the mood for a great conversation. As you find your seat in a quiet corner of the shop, your date looks you straight in the eye and says, "I would like to get to know you."

Believe it or not, most sales interactions can feel this exhilarating at the beginning. Think about the last time you wanted to purchase a big-ticket item, such as jewelry, a new dress or a tailored suit, a popular electronic device, or maybe a car. As you enter the store or walk through the parking lot and see all the beautiful merchandise, your inner child is awakened, and you are ready to explore the possibilities. So if most buying experiences begin this way, the question we must answer is, "What went wrong?" Let's go back to the coffee shop!

After your date has expressed that he or she would like to get to know you, you begin saying a little bit about yourself, being mindful to not give away too much too early. Everything seems good, but about a minute into your brief self-narrative, your date interrupts you. Okay, no problem; he or she is simply excited to realize that you both have something in common. Then your date continues to talk…and talk…*and talk*!

Your date's voice has now drowned out the jazz music, and hearing your date laugh at his or her own jokes sounds like plates being thrown against the coffee-shop wall. He or she occasionally asks you one closed-end question, which only requires one word to answer, in order to sip some coffee and then immediately begin talking again. After thirty minutes of this, you are ready to leave, and your date is unsure why. As you walk out, he or she says ignorantly, "I thought we were getting to know each other!"

Similar to the coffee-shop scenario, what goes wrong in most sales interactions is that the salesperson learns absolutely nothing about the customer that he or she is courting because the salesperson is too busy talking. The salesperson believes that he or she is building rapport by filling the silence with his or her voice. If the salesperson finds one thing he or she has in common with the customer, the salesperson hangs onto it for dear life as if it's the ticket to the "yes" train. The customer can sense the ingenious effort by the salesperson and labels this action as being salesy, which further perpetuates the stigma regarding sales.

The most effective method to building rapport is to learn more about the person with whom you are speaking. Your goal should not be just to find one thing that you have in common, but to discover more about your customer's unique situation. Some salespeople feel like they have to say things that are not true about themselves to make a connection, but that is deceptive and not an effective way to build rapport. *Most people try to find something and forget to discover something about the customer.*

This approach causes you to look only at the external attributes of a customer or refer to negative stereotypes when trying to relate. The fact that your customer is male or female or from another country can be substantial, but not enough in itself in helping us build rapport. Connecting with a particular customer requires us to tap into the person's real character to understand him or her sincerely.

Begin with the End in Mind

You can learn a lot about asking questions by watching a good attorney perform a cross-examination on a witness. The attorney always knows where he or she wants to land but does not reveal it until later in the cross-examination. The attorney asks a series of questions that lead down the desired path and uncover pertinent information. Think about your product and its features when forming your questions. Ask well-thought-out questions to minimize the number of questions you have to ask to obtain the same information.

For example, asking, "What service are you currently using?" and "What don't you like about your current service?" can be replaced by simply asking, "How could your service be better?" If I were selling cars and I wanted to know if my customer will find value in the high gas mileage a particular vehicle provides, I could ask, "What would a typical day driving this car look like?" If you are in real estate and want to know what will attract your customer, you can ask, "Which room in your home do you generally spend most of your time?" Once you get the customers to verbalize their wants and needs, all you have to do is play matchmaker.

Purposeful Questions

Every question should serve a preordained purpose in a sales interaction. Some questions help to understand your customer better; some are to qualify your client for a product, whereas others are used to simply comprehend better. Some questions will reveal how your product will affect the customer's lifestyle, and some will be used to confirm the customer's need for your product. If you combine these questioning techniques with the following method of "taking exits," this will sound like a smooth flowing conversation instead of an interrogation process.

Take Exits

For anyone who has ever been on a road trip, the end goal is always to arrive at your destination safely and within a reasonable time. Nonetheless, there are exits that you take for various reasons. Restroom breaks, buying snacks, sight-seeing, and even to get more directions. These exits can add excitement and adventure to your road trip, which can create lasting memories. The same proves true for a sales conversation. Your goal should be to arrive at a sale, but you can build rapport along the way by taking the natural exits presented to you.

For example, if your customer happens to mention that he or she has to get started on dinner, you can make that an exit by simply asking, "What are you making?" To be more efficient at this, you also want to ask follow-up questions. Examples of good follow-up questions would be, "Is that your favorite dish to make?" or "Where did you learn to cook?"

It is a good idea to add your own experience with cooking your favorite dish if you also share an interest in the topic, but it should be genuine and brief. This opening is your customer's time to shine, so keep him or her as the focus of your conversation. If you keep the exit brief, you can easily get back on the highway to a sale with a more comfortable and friendly customer.

Rewards of Building Rapport

Your conversations do not have to be long to be effective. If you are only concerned with the additional time it takes to build rapport with your customer, you will miss the rewards of that relationship. "People don't care how much you know until they know how much you care" (John Maxwell). When you build a good rapport with a customer, he or she is not only more likely to buy your product but also more willing to be patient if things go awry.

For example, I had a woman who

demonstrated a high amount of patience when challenges arose during the installation process of her services. Several times, we had to reschedule her appointment, and although it was not the ideal experience for the customer, she said to me, "The only reason I am still going to do this is that I like you." That experience reminded me that the reward for building rapport is trust and loyalty for a salesperson.

Customers will show more loyalty to a salesperson whom they like and trust. If you are in an environment that is highly competitive or you incur charge-backs when a customer cancels, a strong rapport will encourage that customer to keep his or her business with you even if there are hiccups along the way. Phone representatives who have to be mindful of their average call time have commonly expressed that building rapport takes too much time. When I was asked to handle a few escalated supervisor calls for these representatives, I discovered that I took a few more minutes to build rapport, but they doubled their time by arguing with the customer and then having to wait for an available supervisor.

Lifestyle Questions

I am surprised that most people don't ask lifestyle questions while dating or getting to know someone. Unfortunately, we live in a world where you can't take everyone's word at face value. However, is he or she to be blamed if we never asked? At least if you ask, you can then observe to see if people's actions align with their answers to your questions. For those who find sincere and honest partners, these questions help to know their mates more intimately.

Lifestyle questions focus on a customer's activities, interests, and opinions. They are by design more personal to give you more insight into an individual's personality. Uncovering how a person likes to relax, or how he or she thinks or feels about something, speaks to his or her value system. Since people are unique, you can discover things about your customers that can help you position your product as the missing piece to a better experience doing what they already like to do.

Three major areas of a person's life fall into the category of lifestyle questions. These questions will help you learn more about how the customer lives, works, and plays. Considering how your product or service will affect these three areas will help customers see the overall value it can add to their lives. If you are looking for great examples of lifestyle questions, simply take note of some of the questions a doctor asks a patient during a general checkup.

Identify which questions are appropriate for your product, and test them out to see what kind of information you can gather. This process may require some tweaking, but it is a great place to start.

Below are some examples lifestyle questions:

1. What hobbies do you enjoy the most?
2. How do you like to unwind and relax?
3. What do you do for work?
4. Do you enjoy outdoor activities?
5. What do you do for entertainment?

Think Whole House

When talking to a customer, most salespeople only ask questions with the person in front of them in mind. It is very likely in most situations that the customer you are speaking with will not be the only person using the product. When you can uncover the needs of other individuals in the household, it gives the customer added motivation to buy.

When I sold life insurance and financial products for Primerica Financial, the largest distributor in North America, I relied heavily on whole-house questions. Especially since the customer's family would be the primary beneficiaries for the majority of the products we sold. It would be difficult to position the value of a mutual fund without first asking about college plans for the kids or retirement goals that clients have with their spouses.

Considering the impact of the buying decision on other people also helps to win over the spouses if they are not present. Couples usually like to check with one another before making a significant purchase, so including them in the conversation early on prevents the spouses from feeling left out. If your customer wants to hold off the sale to check with his or her spouse, you can ask the customer to call the spouse or remind him or her that you both have carefully considered the needs of the spouse to give the customer the confidence he or she is making the right decision. Sometimes there is no way around it, so be respectful and schedule an appointment if you have to.

Listen Effectively

Listening is a timeless courtesy that will always be an invaluable part of any conversation, but even more valuable in a sales conversation. Most people believe they listen effectively. However, I realize that most people mistake "hearing" people with "listening" to people. We listen at a rate of 125–250 words per minute, but we think at 1,000–3,000 words per minute. Most of the time we hear a few things someone is saying but have already begun to reflect on how we will respond. This behavior is especially unproductive in a sales conversation because it results in developing inaccurate assumptions and misjudgments that can destroy the sale.

Listen effectively by seeking to understand the other person's perspective. Great listeners tend to ask follow-up questions rather than make follow-up comments. Great salespeople know how easy it is to assume you know what someone is going to say, so they make concentrated efforts to stop thinking for the customer and just listen.

Taking Notes

When possible, taking notes of your customer's response to your questions is highly recommended. You will forget about 80 percent of what you do not write down, and if you have to follow up later, you run the risk of forgetting some vital information. After two to five days, that percentage increases and essential information could be missing when it is time for the follow-up appointment. Even immediately after a conversation, we can usually recall only 50 percent of what we heard. Politely asking your client if it is permissible to jot down some notes could be the boost you need to increase your results.

Be mindful not to get so involved with taking notes that you forget to connect with your customers. You do not need to act as a stenographer and write everything down word for word, just key points, names, needs, and concerns that they express. Sales is like playing matchmaker. To find a perfect match, you must have a good understanding of the two parties whom you wish to connect. Instead of matching two people, you are just connecting an individual with a product or service.

First, you must understand your product or service. Your product will serve as your bachelor, whom you are marketing to potential clients. Secondly, you must come to know your customer by using the techniques previously mentioned in this chapter. Understanding your customer will allow you to identify what makes him or her and your specific product a perfect match, and your job is to effectively communicate this and give the customer an idea of a first date. They may not always hit it off, but there is no better feeling than when your product and customer is a match made in Heaven!

There I was, wrestling with the idea of quitting before I had even started. But after seeing the name unknown on the screen, it became clear and most fitting for me to get along. I needed to draw enough interest over time to get in her home; silly me, I was prone to pinning down the wrong targets.

"One of the hardest things for me was to leave before it had even started," she said. "Indeed, if you believe in me, I can fulfill your wildest dreams and lead you the farthest.

"Tell me, how would you like to earn a trip to Belize just you and me just for starters and sip piña coladas under the palm trees as you listen to the symphony of the calm seas and dance while your feet leave prints in the sand like the artist…formally known?"

As I'm listening over the phone, I was hoping for a chance for us to meet again, this *time maybe alone because the last time was hardly spent, but now I could sense the seriousness in her tone—what a drastic turn of events. See, that second meeting turned into a permanent stint, and as we boxed, it became a classic; we were that pair whom everyone watched and was convinced that our love was turning intense. The benefits were immense, so the passion that was burning quickly shifted and she started to vent. The picture that was painted sounded horrific, and it didn't make any sense.*

She told me to listen as she tried to explain that if we wanted to sustain it, then we needed to learn how to split. "I beg your pardon, my darling, but I'm not buying it; I need to know why."

-The Heart of Sales

Chapter 4
Best of My Love

Social Media QR Codes

Every good relationship is good because the two individuals realize the value that their partner brings to their life. Whether it is how one partner keeps the family together or how the other provides, each brings something to the table. When a partner feels valued, it builds intimacy and trust in that relationship.

Although every relationship has its bumps and bruises, a good relationship should make life easier and better. When someone does not feel valued or see the value added by his or her spouse, the relationship is doomed to fail. It is important to identify what value someone brings to your life before making a serious commitment, which helps you communicate your appreciation appropriately.

Know Your Value

"Value" is defined as "the regard that something deserves; the importance, worth, or usefulness to someone." Dictionary.com

To demonstrate the value of your product, you must do it with confidence. When you express confidence seen and felt, it increases credibility. You must have confidence in two things when selling. You must have confidence in your product, and, even more importantly, you must have confidence in yourself. You cannot have one without the other and expect to experience lasting success.

Your Product

When you are knowledgeable about your product, people will see your confidence. The easiest way to becoming more knowledgeable about a product is to use it! The more you know about your product, the more confident you will be during your sales interactions. A personal experience will help you display a genuine excitement about your product that becomes contagious to customers.

Think about how excited you are when you tell a friend about a great movie, book, or restaurant. The enthusiasm and confidence you display when recommending that thing is through the roof without even trying. Your personal experience serves as the ignition that drives that person to take your recommendation.

If you are in a position where that is not possible, you can build confidence in your product by reading reviews or using testimonials from customers who have a personal experience with your product. For example, a Realtor who is well informed about the exciting details of a particular home and community will be more effective in communicating the value to his or her potential buyer.

When I was selling my home a few years ago, I observed as a real-estate agent brought a potential buyer to see my home. The agent stood at the door the entire time as the couple walked around the house freely. As the homeowner, I was a little uneasy with strangers touring my home unaccompanied, but my sales mind-set was even more troubled. Why would someone waste time to drive a client to a home and not take the opportunity to learn more about the customer?

Knowing what is on the market and being familiar with it can only help you when the right customer shows up. When a customer sees that you do not know your product or that you are disengaged, you tell the customer nothing about "your product" and a lot about "your other product," which is yourself. Always remember that the product has a brand and you have a brand. Consumers may still want to purchase a specific brand name, but they don't have to do it with you. When business owners, entrepreneurs, and sales professionals demonstrate that they value their customers, their results will skyrocket!

You Are the Product

Have you ever met a man or a woman who on the outside was like a gift from God? A physically attractive person who maybe even looked great on paper, having a good career or education. However, the way the individual represented him- or herself made an instantly undesirable impression. Ignorance and arrogance can make the most beautiful things look ugly.

We have all heard the saying that "the

product sells itself." Although that may be true for some products, most products will require a skilled representative to position it correctly. That is also why salespeople are some of the highest paid professionals in the workforce. Every successful salesperson knows that the first product that a customer buys, is you! When a customer buys you, he or she is more likely to listen to what you have to sell. So how do you build self-confidence in sales and remove doubt?

First, you must understand and accept that sales is a numbers game. This understanding will help you to maintain a balanced perspective when you do not make the sale. Also, understanding the numbers will keep you from adopting a negative attitude with your customers. No salesperson no matter how good makes 100 percent of the shots he or she attempts. On the other side, if you do not shoot, you will miss every time. "You will miss 100 percent of the shots you don't attempt" (Wayne Gretzky).

Make sure you understand the numbers associated with your product. Learn how many noes you should expect to receive a yes! There is no way around the numbers game, so do not lose confidence, and do not get angry when someone says no. If everyone said yes, then why would the company need you? What then would be your value?

Secondly, you must learn to appreciate the process. Just like any other skill in life, selling is a skill that requires refinement. You must allow yourself to make mistakes, but commit to learning from them. If you remain flexible to learning new methods, you will build confidence in your abilities as a sales professional.

Write down things that you could have done better, ask others whom you trust to share what is working for them, and then practice. Role-playing with a family member or a friend is a good way to expedite the learning process and can help you to discover areas you may need to work on the most. The toughest thing for some people to accept regarding a sales position is that it is primarily commission. However, a person with the heart of sales can overcome that fear by being knowledgeable. Salespeople love the fact that their effort determines their income. They confidently take the commission challenge because they believe in their product, themselves!

Features

Tell the truth! There is a physical feature that gets you every time. Is it the height, the eyes, the lips, the muscles, the shape, the feet, the dimples, the teeth, the shoulders? This list of possibilities could go on and on, but I think you get the point. It is natural for us as humans to be attracted to specific features in people. I believe that not only should we be aware of this fact, but we should accept it. Me personally, I'm an ankle guy. I love a woman with strong and sexy ankles! A woman's ankle lets me know if I will be able to lean on her. But seriously, you must know what features of your product attracts certain customers.

"Bells and whistles" is a term that has been most popular when talking about the features of a product. Faithful to the phrase, hearing about the features a product comes with definitely rings in a customer's ear. Whether it is just a few or too much to count, every product has features. Customers want the most for their money, and sometimes the number of features offered is the deciding factor between two similar products, but simply stating the features should not be the primary focus of your presentation.

I realized this when I relocated to Fort Myers, Florida, for my job as a sales trainer. In real estate, features are amenities, but in essence, they are still features of the product. By definition, a feature is a distinctive attribute or aspect of something. Your product demonstrates that it has unique features. Some of the features that weighed most on my decision were the washer/dryer, the clubhouse, the lake view, and the overall location. These features instantly caught my attention and made me want to learn more about the property. Your product's features are what attracts your customer and spark his or her curiosity to learn more.

The first step to making a powerful product presentation or PPP is to know your product's features. You cannot expect a customer to take you seriously or view you as a professional if you are not knowledgeable about what you are selling. Product knowledge comes through formal training provided by your company or by embarking on a journey of self-learning. Remember, a feature is a distinctive attribute, so you will need to understand what makes your product different from similar products in the market. Different does not necessarily mean better, and it does not have to be. Customers are different and do not place the same value on things, so when you know what's different about your product, you can then understand what makes it better for your particular customer.

A fatal mistake that most salespeople make is that they overwhelm the customer with too many features during their presentation. In the sales world, this is called "data dumping." Remember the date in the coffee shop from the previous chapter? You don't want to become the person who just talks and talks. Too much information tends to complicate a sale and can overwhelm your customers. You must learn as much as you can about your product so that you can select which features will have the most value and present it to them. The features you choose to highlight can change from one customer to another, so learn to treat each person and every opportunity uniquely.

Once you arrive at this point of making your presentation, you are directly drawing from what you have learned about your customer and connecting it to what you know about your product. Become the professional "matchmaker." This skill will help you avoid making the mistake of drowning your customer's buying energy with useless information and overcomplicating the sale process.

Benefits

Every product has a feature, and every feature has a benefit. A benefit is an advantage or profit gained from a product or service. If you tell customers about your product's features but never go deeper to show them what the benefit of that feature is, you shortchange your presentation. What advantage does a particular feature add to your product? What will that feature allow your customers to do that they were not able to do before? How does that feature differentiate your product from its competitors? As the saying goes, "*Features* tell. Benefits sell."

My new home had great features that appealed to me, but I have yet to mention *why* those features stood out. The washer/dryer prevented me from having to go to a laundromat. The clubhouse had a community gym, pool, Jacuzzi, a full kitchen, and a billiard room. These features meant that residents did not have to leave the community to exercise or relax. The lake view was important because it provided great scenery, and lastly the location was close to my job and had multiple shopping plazas nearby.

Think about some of the best purchases you have made. What were the features that appealed to you the most and what were some of the other features that did not have as much influence on your buying decision? What benefit did you gain by using your favorite features? Although you may not have found much use for some other features of the product, what benefit would someone else receive if he or she used that feature?

Someone once shared with me an experience he had while buying a car. The person explained to me how the salesperson spent a lot of time highlighting the heated seats in a particular car. This feature was something that apparently impressed the seller but held no value for the customer. It is not that heated seats are a bad feature, but the salesperson seemed to forget that he was selling cars in Florida. In a state that rarely gets real winter weather, heated seats are not at the top of the priority list when purchasing a car. If the customer had said that he had back problems, the heated seats might have been a hit, but that was not the case in this particular scenario.

Some salespeople make the mistake of giving too much information, but others make the critical error of only sharing information that appears to be important to them. You may buy a particular type of car for the horsepower because you like power and speed, but someone else may purchase that same vehicle because of the safety features or style. Understanding the benefits of a feature will move you closer to positioning the value for your customer. A great salesperson is a great listener and always has the customer's best interests in mind. Aim to serve your customer sincerely, and it will help you avoid selling to only your preferences.

Value

Once you have highlighted the features that will appeal most to your customer and have educated your customer on the benefits of that feature, you can now paint the picture of how that feature will add value to your customer's life. A value statement takes a general benefit and makes it specific to a customer's lifestyle. If a person can visualize himself or herself using a product, it makes it easier for that person to understand the value of having the product.

Now think back to the benefits I shared about my new home. Would a billiard room and gym be a selling factor if I was not interested in playing pool or exercising? Of course not! When I walked into the clubhouse, I was able to visualize myself using it, and that increased the value. If the Realtor had asked lifestyle questions and discovered that I like to compete against my younger brother Steve in pool, a value statement would simply be, "Since the clubhouse has a billiard room, you and your brother Steve can enjoy a little friendly competition."

The lake view was more than just great scenery for me. I knew it would be one of the first places I would go after a long day of work to unwind. An example value statement could be "After a long day of sales training, you can relax on your patio and enjoy the serenity of your lake view."

Finally, the location was convenient because it was close to work and nearby shopping plazas. A great value statement would have been, "Since you're so close to work, you can grab some lunch from one of the local restaurants and enjoy it while viewing the lake." The Realtor missed opportunities to build value, but I still said yes because I naturally think about value when purchasing a product. Most customers will not make those connections because the product does not always sell itself, but you do! Paint the picture.

In 2017, FOX charged companies around $5 million for a thirty-second ad during the Super Bowl. With 114 million viewers tuning in the year prior, there is no wonder why companies dish out this kind of money to present their best commercials. Outrageous prices for an advertising commercial instantly become the norm because of the value companies receive from the event. People who are not fans of the sport admit to only watching the Super Bowl for the half-time show and the outrageous commercials.

TV commercials do an excellent job of

painting a picture of the experience a customer will have with the product advertised. Some commercials are realistic and accurate, while others exaggerate for humor or impact. Your value statement should have the same impact or even greater because you are not speaking to a general audience, but rather a specific person.

Use descriptive language and action words that speak to a customer's senses. Terms such as "picture," "imagine," "see," "focus," or "notice" will stimulate a customer's visual senses. Words such as "feel," "warm," "cozy," and "relaxed" will talk to his or her kinesthetic senses. Sensory words will help you to paint a beautiful picture of the experience customers can have if they were to say yes. Features tell you about the attributes of the product and benefits tell you what advantages those features provide, but value inserts your product into customers' reality and helps them see it for themselves.

Price versus Value

Price is what you pay; Value is what you get.

—Warren Buffet

The topic of value is combined with the conversation on price. You will often hear jewelry dealers speak about price using the term value. The Cullinan Diamond is 3,106,750 karats and is valued at $400 million. Contrary to what some salespeople believe, value does not compete against price; value justifies the price. The more value you build, the higher the price the product can command. Salespeople who lean on price as their key selling point fail to understand the art of sales.

Although the Cullinan Diamond is precious, it is only the third most expensive diamond in the world. The two most expensive diamonds in the world are the Sancy diamond, which is part of the French Crown Jewel Collection, and the

Koh-i-Noor diamond, which is the property of the British Crown. Both stones have a value that is unestimated, or in other words, priceless. No one can purchase them because the owners have deemed that no price will justify the value it holds for them.

Similarly, your customer may not be wealthy; however, there will be some things he or she considers priceless. Specific areas considered are a customer's family's safety, peace of mind, health, and time. When you can communicate how your product influences what your customer holds to be priceless, the topic of price becomes easier to discuss. More than likely, your product is not as rare as these majestic diamonds, so the price is still a topic because of the competition. Nonetheless, you put yourself in a much better position when you focus on value.

Know Your Why

"People often say that motivation doesn't last. Well, neither does bathing—that's why we recommend it daily."

—Zig Ziglar

Many times, people focus on why they would not enter into another relationship or love again after a failed relationship. "Why would I want to be vulnerable again?" "Why would I put myself in the position to get hurt again or fail again?" Instead, I would ask you to focus on why you would. The possibility of finding a lifelong partner or enjoying a healthy relationship when maximized is enough motivation to push you past your previous failures.

Do you know why you want to accomplish what you want to achieve? You establish your why by knowing what motivates you even when you don't feel motivated. Many things motivate us to strive for success. Your methods of motivation should be easy to access. These elements include positive affirmations, music, prayer, meditation, visual aids, money, power, and so on. Most people understand that they will need some motivation to be successful at anything, but many do not go deeper to know what their why truly is.

Motivation provides a powerful yet temporary boost in energy that can help you stay focused on the task. Your why does not just motivate you; it inspires you! "Why" is something you internalize and becomes the driving force behind your effort. To discover your "why" you have to be more specific about your goals and understand the impact that achieving your goals will have on others.

One of the pictures on my vision board at home is of different fruit smoothies laid out on a concession stand. One of my whys is to help my mother retire from a daily job and start her own smoothie business. This objective is one of the reasons why I work the way I do. Another picture on that board is the private school that I want my son to attend. It is another reason why I wake up every morning and strive to give my best every day.

Your why should be bigger than you. The more specific your why is and the more people it affects, the more effective your why will be. Whom would you like to help when you reach your goal? How will achieving your goal change their lives in the long term?

If you haven't already done so, take time to create a vision board today. Be specific about your goals and find pictures that reflect your objective. If you want to buy a house, do not stop at how many bedrooms or bathrooms. Ask yourself where it will be? Will you need a big kitchen so that you can host your family for Thanksgiving? Will it need to have a pool big enough for all the kids in your family to play? Your 'Why' does not have to be extravagant, it just needs to speak to your values.

The scene played out like a movie: her running out and me chasing behind, refusing to let her go, which usually means someone's trying. Though back and forth we go until the knots were loosened and started untying, I'm sweating profusely 'cause I was thrown for a doozy when she said that she needed some time.

I'm thinking needing some time was something used loosely for those who couldn't make up their minds, but didn't you choose me; see, I was about to leave when you called and said you'd like to meet to further discuss the designs.

But what about trust? You know, I should've stuck to my gut when I first saw the big bucks on the design instead of backing up. I should've had enough tucked away in a safe where I didn't have to pay any attention when she rolled up from behind.

But I hung around like suspensions, and now I'm trying not to burn all these bridges that were lifted above troubled waters in my mind. Remember the last time that we kicked it? I said that I thought I was sort of trippin' 'cause I started falling for you to the point that I was almost convicted and now this is…what it's coming to?

"It's complicated," she says. I was persistent in finding the truth. I even thought about what I could do different, but then I was reminded that resistance was a part of the school. Sometimes you have to dismiss it to really find if it's true love, and if that is what this is then the intense heat is what makes this unique diamond a jewel.

-The Heart of Sales

Chapter 5
It's Complicated

Social Media QR Codes

Whether you are in a relationship or single, one of the toughest things to encounter is rejection. Being accepted is a basic human emotion, so the act of rejection is something people want to avoid. Men do not approach women they have feelings for from fear of rejection, and women are frightened to start new relationships because of past rejection.

Even within the borders of a relationship, rejection can be present. If a husband rejects his wife's cooking, she can become discouraged and even refuse to make another attempt. One thing that we must understand and accept is that we all will encounter rejection in life. Although being accepted is a basic human emotion, saying no is also a natural human reaction. Many times, we say no in a relationship without actually understanding the situation.

If we learn not to take rejection personally, we can overcome it and use it as an opportunity to find out more about each other. Sales can feel complicated at times, but if you build your understanding, you will develop competence.

Rejection Is Not Final

"Rejection is the dismissing or refusal of a proposal, idea, and so on." Dictionary.com

Understand the objection

Similar to a relationship, a customer can give you an objection at any time during the sales conversation. It can come early in the conversation or later on down the line, but the most important thing is that you understand the true nature of the objection. Uncover why the customer is rejecting your offer before trying to overcome it. Without knowing the actual opposition, you could be directing your efforts in the wrong area.

I grew up in South Florida where it is normal to see artificial plastic ducks floating in a community pond or lake. As a child and even in my adult years, I never understood why they were there. I thought that maybe it was to beautify the lake or attract other ducks, until one of my students in my sales class revealed it to me. She explained to me that her father worked for the city, and those ducks are used to help city workers locate the drainage pipe that was beneath the water. This explanation instantly connected with me on how to handle objections in a sales interaction.

A customer will give you an objection that is very general, and it acts just like the artificial duck in a lake. To overcome an objection, you must first uncover what is beneath the surface to clarify what the actual objection is. There is probably more to the story, and if you give up after rejection, you halt the progress you made during your conversation. You are not going to let a fake duck stop you, are you?

Most people understand this truth about the real objection being beneath the surface because they have experienced it within a dating relationship. Just think back to the last time you asked a mate, "What's wrong?" and he or she replied in an apparently upset tone of voice, "Nothing!" It can take a little time and persistence before an angry partner finally opens up to express his or her feelings. Similarly, customers do not always say why they are hesitant to move forward, and a little persistence, not pushiness, can carry you over the hump.

Reading Your Customer

Sales can be like a chess match where you have to pay attention to nonverbal communication just as much, if not more, as you do verbal communication. Only, in sales your opponent is not the individual sitting across from you, but the obstacles that you need to overcome with your customers so that you can reach an agreement, and they can enjoy the benefits of your product. Likewise, dating can sometimes feel like a chess match as well. Your ability or inability to read the other person's body language can be the difference between a checkmate or game over.

At times, I enjoy just sitting at a local bar and watching how people communicate and interact. Noticing the constant stares of a man at a particular woman and then seeing her response to his blatant signals can be very telling. If she continues to give eye contact, it may be the green light the man needs to come over and introduce himself.

However, if she turns her back or moves to another part of the bar, it should be enough to communicate to the man that she is not interested. Rejection normally occurs when the man has not picked up any of her body language.

Being attentive enough to read your customers requires focus. Your customers communicate their emotions of skepticism, uncertainty, or fear in various ways. Reading your customers' body language, verbiage, tone, and facial expressions are essential to your success. Even concerns that are not verbalized require you to respond.

While training a new door-to-door sales representative in a residential neighborhood, I witnessed what happens when we do not read the customer's body language. After the sales rep had knocked on the door, I stepped back to allow him to engage the customer alone. As I observed the interaction from a close distance, I noticed subtle changes in the customer's tone and body language. He crossed his arms tightly, stood firmly in the doorway of his home to block the entrance, and had a very skeptical look on his face. His eyes squinted, and his eyebrows slightly rose as he toggled his attention back and forth between the sales rep and me. He was saying a lot without words, but the sales rep did not read it.

When the sales rep mentioned our home-security product and began asking probing questions about how the customer protects his home, the customer immediately shut down! I could see it clearly, but the sales rep was blind to the fact that the customer was skeptical of who we were.

During their conversation, I overheard the customer say that he was from Seattle. At that time, we were a month away from Super Bowl XLIX in which the Seattle Seahawks were scheduled to play the New England Patriots. I seized the opportunity to mention the Deflate Gate scandal that surrounded the New England Patriots and asked the customer for his opinion. Immediately, his arms came down, his facial expression relaxed, and for the first time, he spoke to us as if he was talking with good friends.

As I heard the customer share his views and watched a smile form on his face as he discussed how his team could win the game, I knew that everyone should learn to read the customer. It is not a complicated process that requires an extensive sales background; you just have to pay attention and respond. Share facts that add credibility. If your customer seems skeptical and unsure of your intentions, share how he or she will benefit. If customers show excitement and interest in a particular feature of the product, spend more time talking about that feature.

During that same Super Bowl, one of the most memorable plays occurred on the last play of the game. It was the play that would change the outcome of the game and one that Seahawks fans would love to forget ever happened. As the Seattle Seahawks lined up on the one-yard line with what looked like the game was in their pocket, Malcolm Butler of the New England Patriots read the eyes and body language of the quarterback perfectly.

Instead of handing the ball to their pro-bowl caliber running back Marshawn Lynch, the Seahawks opted to throw a pass, which was intercepted by Butler. The game was over on that play! Tom Brady and the New England Patriots were crowned champions because of Malcolm Butler's attention to body language.

Be Persistent Instead of Pushy

I remember when my firstborn, Josiah, started learning how to speak; he went through a phase where the answer to every question I asked him was "No!" It did not matter what the question was; the response was always the same. I wanted to see if he understood what he was saying or if this was just a habit. I started asking him if he wanted things like candy, ice cream, juice, and toys. I asked him everything that I knew he loved and would want. Time after time, he responded with a stern and confident "No!"

As I pondered on this story, I realized that we are not that much different as adults. Granted, we can comprehend what someone is asking, and we think that our first response is our answer, but many times, it is not. How many times have you seen someone asked at a fast-food restaurant, "Would you like ketchup or mustard?" and the reply is "No. Well you know on second thought, maybe just a little?" You may have been at a friend's house and were asked, "Can I get you something to drink?" and your initial response was "No, I'm fine." Only to say a few moments later, "Actually, I will take some water." It appears that our programming is to say no, but it is not always the final answer; usually it's our "second thought."

This syndrome presents an exciting challenge for all salespeople, but especially those who do not want to come off as being pushy. I believe the difference lies in how you choose to approach the rejection. Salespeople who are pushy ignore what the customer has said and fire off a barrage of selling points in an attempt to push the sale forward. If they do ask questions, their questions do not seek to understand the customer's objection, but rather demean a person's initial decision. Their tone of voice can add to the ineffectiveness of their strategy because they are usually defensive as result of the rejection.

When all has failed, some salespeople revert to sarcastic comments that do nothing but upset the customer further. Comments like "I guess you don't like to save money" or "Maybe your wife wears the pants" are examples of the counterproductive things pushy salespeople might say.

Being persistent only means that you do not give up trying to understand your customer after the first objection. Asking some open-ended questions that encourage customers to elaborate on the reason for their objection is pivotal in these moments. If you actively listen, you should be able to tie in the value you previously uncovered to help overcome their objection. There is no magic number on how many questions you can ask, so you should be attentive to customers' tone and body language to know when enough is enough.

Below are some examples of open-ended questions to help understand an objection:

1. What concerns do you have?
2. What would make you more comfortable about buying this product?
3. What concerns do you have that's preventing you from moving forward?
4. How can I earn your business?
5. Can you tell me more about (said objection)?

Overcoming Early Objections

I recall that when I was in high school, I saw a beautiful young lady cross my line of sight. I was very shy, but after a few days and some fear of loss (which you will learn about later), I was ready to shoot my shot. When I approached her, the conversation appeared to be going well until I asked her for her number. She simply paused for a second and abruptly said, "Nope!" I was confused, disappointed, and even a little embarrassed that I had been rejected. *To be continued...*

When objections come at the beginning of the sales conversation, we handle them differently because they are a different kind of objection. Typically, the customer is not objecting to the product but to the continuation of the sales conversation. These initial objections can be difficult to overcome and sometimes hard to not take personally. The first thing you must accept is that nothing will work 100 percent of the time. Remember that sales is undoubtedly a numbers game, but some techniques can swing the odds back in your favor.

Speaking of "back in your favor," let's go back to my high-school crush. After her initial rejection, I noticed that we had a few common friends, and throughout the week we would be in the same group conversations. Gradually we began talking more and branching off to have our own conversations. One Friday as I walked her to the area where the school busses were, she crumpled up a small piece of paper and placed it in my hand. After she walked away, I opened it to discover that she had given me her telephone number. *To be continued…*

Eight-Mile Strike

More commonly known as addressing the elephant in the room, this is an excellent method that can help prevent an initial objection before the statement. I call this technique, the eight-mile strike. In the movie *8 Mile*, the main character B-Rabbit, played by the rapper Eminem, has to compete against a foe in a rap battle. Eminem's friend Cheddar Bob reminds him that his opponent will use some of the adverse occurrences that Eminem previously experienced against him. Eminem decides to strip his opponent of this ammunition by making his whole rap about those negative experiences, which made it challenging for his competition to use them. His plan works perfectly, leaving his opponent speechless because it would have been pointless for him to repeat the same occurrences Eminem used.

The eight-mile strike is canceling out a negative before it happens by simply being the first to say it. Some early objections are visible from miles away. Acknowledge the possible objection before the customer, and he or she usually will not use it to avoid sounding redundant. For example, saying, "I can tell that you are in a rush, so I won't keep you long" is an excellent way to buy some time to present your specials in a fast-paced retail environment. This method also works well when there are objections that are familiar to your product. For example, a life-insurance salesperson could start his or her interaction by saying, "I know you don't plan on dying anytime soon and don't see the need for life insurance right now." This technique will help you to strike first, instead of striking out before you even start.

K.I.S.S versus K.I.L.L

The fatal error that most people make when responding to an objection is they simply talk too much. A long-drawn-out response to a simple objection causes the customer to disengage, and the salesperson can begin to sound less confident. Remember the K.I.S.S versus K.I.L.L technique whenever you are responding to an objection: Keep It Short and Simple rather than Keeping It Long and Lengthy. Your responses to an objection should be direct and to the point. Address the concern, highlight the value of continuing the conversation, and move forward.

Feel, Felt, Found

Overcoming objections is not a skill only for salespeople who can think quickly on their feet. Anyone can master this skill after learning the right techniques. This last method is so simple to use but will make you look like an expert at overcoming objections. Feel, Felt, Found is a three-step process to overcome objections and is very effective. The next time you receive an objection from a customer or are in a disagreement with your significant other, follow the steps below.

Feel— "I understand how you feel" indicates that you understand a person's objection. Stating that you understand how he or she feels demonstrates empathy. Empathy helps you to see the situation from the other person's point of view. This response shows customers that you are listening and that you acknowledge their concerns rather than ignoring them.

Felt— "I have customers who felt the same way," which expresses that other people have felt the same way and uses the Jones effect (which you will learn later) to ensure the customer does not feel alone in his or her thinking. The famous phrase "safety in numbers" is genuine, and people consider how others might have felt about an opportunity when making a buying decision. This truth is the reason why movies and restaurants either fail or succeed—because of how people rated their experience. This statement also reassures your customers that whatever solution you present takes account of their concerns.

Found— "Until they found out that _____," stating what others discovered or found, speaks to the realization others before them came to after giving it a second thought. This stage is where you would insert the solution to their objection, which can be a highlight of the value others enjoyed because they said yes. Your "found" statement should address their particular concern and provide facts on why that concern is not insurmountable.

You are more than a conqueror, you are an overcomer!

You cannot give up when you face obstacles in life, and you cannot just walk away when an obstacle faces you in sales. Many people quit on great sales opportunities because a challenge is presented. These are moments when you need to remember your why. Your why can motivate you to climb any mountain that stands between you and your goal. In sales, it is commonly referred to as having a tough skin, but the mind-set does not apply only to someone seeking a career in sales. Anything worth having in life requires you to have a tough skin, so do not believe the misperception that you will be able to avoid it if you avoid sales.

What if Thomas Edison lost faith after his 999th failed attempt to invent the lightbulb? Can you imagine how many times he must have heard, "Give up, Thomas! It will never work!" Though Edison when asked said, "I didn't fail 1,000 times. The lightbulb was an invention that required a 1,000 steps." What *if* you are only one attempt away from success? Edison concludes by saying that "Great success is built on failure, frustration, even catastrophe."

Remember my high-school crush? We began dating shortly after the day she gave me her phone number and had a beautiful puppy-love experience. We were dating for about six months, in love, with no foreseeable obstacles ahead. Then one day she informed me that she had to move to New Jersey the next day. I was so crushed. I remember riding my bike about ten miles to her home to say good-bye. We may have been just teenagers, but the hurt was one that I would remember even in adult years. *To be continued...*

One day I was playing Connect Four with a young man called CJ, whom I mentor with the Big Brothers Big Sisters organization. We reached a point in the game that no matter where I put my chip, I would lose. Sometimes in life, no matter which way you look at it, failure is inevitable! The law of failure states, "Failure is to be expected and accepted" because nothing exciting ever happens unless we take risks.

Once the game was over, CJ slid a tab at the bottom, which let all the chips fall on the table so that we could start a completely new game. Seeing that taught me that although failure is inevitable, failure is not final! Some of the greatest people in history have experienced terrible failure in their lives, but their faith helped them to persevere past their hardships.

Nelson Mandela once said, "The greatest glory in living lies not in never failing, but in rising every time we fall." At some point, if you keep trying, life will eventually slide the tab at the bottom and let the chips fall on the table so that you can start a new game! The potential income that is possible because of sales can help you change your life dramatically. It does not matter what circumstance you find yourself in or what mountain stands before you, and you must remember that you are more than a conqueror, you are an overcomer.

They say if you can't stand the heat, then it's time to leave the kitchen, though what was cooking could've been sweet, but I couldn't bear to eat all of the fixings, especially if I was the only one there in the seat by myself sitting alone. See, I haven't seen her in a minute, and we don't speak on the phone. I've made a living since then, but been experimenting with women who played me for cheap, using me as lemons squeezing my creative juices while I'm building them homes.

It was sweet in the beginning, but then the CD started skipping, and I no longer hear the melody of the song, so I merely listened to the repetition in fear of admitting that it was me all along. I should've played my position a little different instead of switching when I would hear them speak like a poem, using sweet nothings as a leash to draw enough interest to keep me conditioned into sniffing for free when easily I could loan.

Though at the time I didn't want to buy so I simply leased my love to whomever was renting. See, I was prone to enlisting those to occupy my mind, and though it was wrong, I was satisfied as long as there was someone who came to visit. Though I always envisioned that she and I would somehow reunite despite how we ended, it was just a matter of time to allow fate to decide just how it would finish.

So now I'm back at the beginning at the bar. Sitting sipping on this last thing of Guinness, I turned and saw in the distance a beautiful woman with a green dress who had just entered the building...

-The Heart of Sales

Chapter 6
Happily Ever After

Social Media QR Codes

When some people think about love, they think about the butterflies in their stomachs or the euphoric feeling of sharing a first kiss. Although love promotes hugs, flowers, and kisses, the foundation of a love relationship is not material or emotional. The true essence of love and relationship is commitment. It is about making a conscious decision to give your time, energy, and loyalty to your partner. There are days when a person may not feel the emotions caused by love or act in a loving way, but love continues to show through his or her commitment.

Loyalty may be one of the most important aspects of commitment, but it is not the only aspect. In a marriage, the two individuals make a promise to give their time, energy, and loyalty to the other. The impact of looking at love as a daily decision instead of relying on ever-changing emotions is that you will enjoy a lasting and fulfilling relationship. Sales is not a chore or a burden; it is a decision to bet on you. It is a decision that requires commitment. Are you committed?

Make A Commitment

"Commitment is a willingness to give your time and energy to something that you believe in, or a promise." Dictionary.com

ABC

If you are old enough, you might remember passing a note to your crush in school with a simple question that sometimes takes a lot of courage to ask: "Do you like me? Yes or No. Circle one." If you were brilliant, you gave yourself even more chances of success by adding "maybe" as a third option. "Maybe" did not feel as good as a yes, but it did not hurt like getting a no either. Since very early in life, we learn that there had to be a question asked or proposal made and a decision made to move toward commitment.

If a person received the note back and it was marked "Yes," it meant that that person probably had a new boyfriend or girlfriend. This action was a pivotal moment for this new relationship, but there were probably signs leading up to this point. The boy throwing paper at the girl and the girl pretending as if she did not like it was all part of the process. Sales is very similar.

"Always be closing" is a familiar phrase when mentioning the closing step of the sales process, and it is very accurate. The whole point of beginning a sales conversation is to arrive at this point eventually, but you cannot wait until you reach this step to communicate that to your customer. In every step of the sales conversation, you should be reinforcing this goal by intentionally infusing statements that point to this objective. When you do this effectively, your customer will not be surprised when you ask for the sale, and you would have eliminated some of the anxiety some feel when approaching this grand finale.

One method you can leverage is speaking in past tense or post sale language. This method is when you relay information as if the customer has already agreed on taking your recommendation. For example, when you are in the discovery step of the sales conversation and asking questions to understand better your customers' needs, this technique can be a huge boost to the customers' buying temperature.

Instead of asking a customer, "How will this service benefit you and your family," you can rephrase it to say, "Once you receive this service, how do you see you and your family using it?" The first part of the statement communicates to the customer that you are confident he or she will be taking your recommendation. You can also do this as you are educating your customer on the features of the product during your presentation.

For example, if I am selling an electronic device that needs to receive updates via the web to work correctly, I could say to the customer, "When you get home, connect to your Wi-Fi for you to receive the latest updates." Once you begin using this type of assumptive language in your sales conversation, you will notice your customers' buying temperature much sooner.

Sense of Urgency

Another method that can be used to "always be closing" is to create a sense of urgency. Consumers are more likely to make a buying decision if there is a time restriction. Think about commercials and advertisements that you have seen that say things like "One-Day Sale" or "Limited Time Offer." Another example is the Black Friday shopping frenzy that happens the day after Thanksgiving in the United States. Granted, people rush to department stores because they anticipate receiving significant discounts and an early start on their Christmas shopping, but the time factor also plays a major role.

You can use this method without the fear of sounding cheesy and artificial by intentionally using words like "today," "right now," "expired," "at this moment," "limited," "exclusive," "this week," "your time," and "immediately." When customers do not feel a sense of urgency to buy something, they delay the purchase and eventually talk themselves out of it or purchase it later from somewhere else. Capitalize on your opportunity by creating a sense of urgency because you may not get another chance.

Fear of Loss

Have you ever returned to a store to purchase something that you saw previously, just to find out it is out of stock? On the other hand, have you found an item you wanted and realized that it was the last one left? In the first example, there was probably an instant feeling of disappointment and maybe even fear that you would not find the product. The second example frequently ignites excitement and may make you feel special that you were lucky enough to get the last one. Fear of loss causes these emotions.

Michael Jordan is one of the best at using this sales strategy to keep a loyal and almost everlasting customer base. Michael

Jordan's shoe brand is famous for its sneakers. The brand has transcended generations and is highly sought out by kids who have never watched him perform. How does this happen? Aside from his highly successful basketball career, great shoe designs, and cult-like following, his understanding of fear of loss also plays a significant role. Jordan only releases a limited number of shoes in each store, and consumers have sometimes had to win tickets even to have a chance to purchase the sneakers. He also only releases one version, in one color at a time. This intentional manipulation of supply and demand causes frenzy for consumers looking to get a pair of Air Jordan sneakers.

I mentioned earlier that fear of loss played a role in getting me to finally approach my high-school crush. This was because I took a few days to contemplate how I would approach her, but never took action due to the fact that I had never approached a girl. A "friend" at the time, and I use that term loosely, said, "If you don't talk to her, I will." Immediately I had the impulse to finally make my move. I made a decision because I could not risk losing her and that fear of loss helped me do something I really wanted to do.

To keep your customers' buying temperature high, you can explore things about your product that create fear of loss. Maybe your supply is not limited, but it is in high demand. Inform your customer throughout your interaction of strong demand for the product and the rate in which it is selling.

If your product has multiple versions and you are positioning one of the more traditional versions, express to your customer the popularity of the one you are presenting. You have heard phrases like "They are flying off the shelves," "One of a kind," and "While supplies last." Use some of these phrases or create some of your own, but no matter what, generate fear of loss.

The Jones Effect

Have you ever tried a new restaurant, but you were not sure of what to order? As you looked over the entire menu for the third time, you probably did one of a few things. You began to examine the items marked as their most favorite dishes with other customers or you just finally asked your server, "What do you recommend?" I have even seen people looking around at other customers' meals nearby to ask, "What is that?" If the other person enjoyed his or her meal and sounded excited when explaining what it was, there is a high probability that you will order the same thing. This syndrome is the Jones effect at work.

The Jones effect creates the safety consumers feel when they know that other customers like an individual product. It is the reason why ratings are so important to companies and consumers. Have you ever had a client ask you if you are using the product you are selling? When I was a door-to-door sales representative for a Fortune 50 cable company in Florida, customers would consistently ask me who else in the neighborhood went with my service. This concern became even more useful when the person I previously signed up was someone customers knew or respected, like a police officer or HOA member.

The phrase "keeping up with the Joneses" deals with the aspect of wanting the same or higher quality of products as a neighbor or friend. Therefore, if all my friends have flat-screen HDTVs, I may not get the same brand, but it is likely to motivate me to get a comparable TV. It all still boils down to the Jones effect. This technique is a very efficient method to utilize if you want to always be closing.

Here is how you can incorporate the Jones effect into your conversation. When introducing new information about your service or answering customers' questions, indicate to them that they would not be alone in that decision. "Most customers go with that option," "Everyone likes this version," "Our most popular is," "We get a lot of people asking for this one," are all great examples of how you can input a little Jones effect in your dialogue. When you combine these elements, you will always be closing.

Talking Price

One of the most frightening moments for some salespeople, in particular for those who are new to sales is talking about the price. Many salespeople can hesitate, become nervous, and even try to avoid this portion of the conversation. This method proves to be a fatal error and has caused many salespeople to fumble the sale at the very end. To complete your PPP, you must learn to talk price effectively.

So why do so many people struggle when it comes to talking about price? One reason is that the salesperson does not know the product enough to understand the value it provides a customer. We see here that understanding the concept of value is not just for the customer, but that it also helps the salesperson. When you do not know the value of your product or service, it makes it harder for you to justify the price.

Oddly enough, there is also a price associated with having fulfilled relationships. With love, talking price should not translate to money but rather your standards. What are you willing to accept in exchange for your time, your energy, and your love? Once you understand your value and what you bring to a relationship, you will not settle for low-ball offers. Furthermore, you will not stutter when speaking about your standards because you know your worth and what you had to overcome to get there. Never settle, because the right person will be ecstatic to invest into a life with you and never ask for a discount.

One reason that people fumble when talking price is that they think with their own pockets. "Thinking with your own pockets" is a phrase a sales professional uses when someone communicates price in an unfavorable way because he or she views the price as being high. This action does not take into consideration whether the price is fair or comparable to the competition; it just looks at the cost and reacts. Imagine working at a Ferrari dealership, but you own a Honda. It can be difficult to communicate a $350,000 price confidently when you initially thought that your $35,000 upgraded LX model cost you a pretty penny.

Fortunately, you do not need to buy a Ferrari to sell a Ferrari. You do not need to live in a mansion to sell a mansion. You do not have to be able to afford your product to sell your product. All you need to do is gain the right perspective and stop thinking with your pockets. What you find to be expensive, your customer may not. Simply build value and present the price in a confident manner.

Let your customer be the judge, not your personal budget.

The final reason a salesperson may fumble when talking price is nothing more than fear, fear that the customer will faint or run away screaming in disbelief. Although it sounds funny, these extreme images play in a salesperson's mind. We assume the worst, imagine the disaster, and the customer begins to feel the energy seeping through our pores. You have to be mindful of the environment you are creating around price because the customer responds to your energy. If you are fearful and nervous, then your customer becomes wary of what is coming next. You put the customer on high alert that something bad is coming his or her way.

One way of staying calm is to recap the value before revealing the price. Hearing how much value they will get from your product will help you and customers keep things in perspective. Sales is a numbers game, meaning that not everyone will say yes to your product no matter what the price is. Once you accept this reality, it allows you to develop a more indifferent attitude and much-needed tough skin. Sales professionals understand that talking about price is inevitable and unavoidable, so it does not make sense to be fearful or try to avoid it. If you know it is coming, all you need is an effective technique so that you feel prepared. "People don't plan to fail; they just fail to plan" (John Beckley).

Technique

When it comes to techniques involving the discussion of price, there is no need to recreate the wheel because there are many successful methods you can quickly adapt. For example, the BK Theory or Burger King Theory. You can remember it with the phrase, "Pitch them high; watch them buy. Pitch them low; watch them go."

Most people know it more commonly

as top-down selling. If your item is on sale or there are higher packages available, start with the higher price. This will give you room to move down if the customer happens to say no to your first offer.

This known as the Burger King Theory because if you order a meal from BK, they will ask you if you want the medium or the large, never mentioning the small option first. Primarily, confidence is nonnegotiable when talking price. If you have done the things I prescribed in the earlier chapters, you should have plenty of motivation and confidence by this point in your interaction.

Power Words

The way we communicate price is the way your customer will receive it. Salespeople can sometimes use a negative tone, which ignites fear and hesitation in the customer of the upcoming price talk. This insecurity frequently happens when a salesperson has a negative perspective of the price. The best way to overcome this is to be aware of word choice and to use positive words when discussing price.

Positive Words and Phrases:

Investment
Best value
Discounted rate
The price is only
Inexpensive advantage

Negative Words and Phrases:

But you have to pay
Extra charge
Cheap
Additional fee
Deal

Also, you should not hesitate or avoid delivering the price. Confidence is vital at this point of the sales interaction, so make sure you say it in a relaxed tone of voice. If there are savings that your customer will benefit from by buying your product, be sure to communicate that also. It may require you to do some math for your customer and write it down so that your customer can see the savings.

Instead of just saying you will save $50 a month, multiply the savings by twelve to show the annual savings your customer will receive from the purchase. When the client learns that he or she will save $600 for the year, it tends to have a bigger impact simply because the number is larger. Whether fear or confidence, whichever you maximize is the emotion that will manifest.

Sometimes the customer is already paying for the service you are offering but with a different company. When your product is more affordable, you should first remind customers of how they will benefit from the value of your service and then explain to them how the switch will be to their financial gain. Everyone is looking for the best value and the least expensive, quality option available to him or her. If you have that, take advantage of the opportunity to crush your competition.

Finally, tie in the savings back to things that are valuable to your customer. If your customer communicated that he or she loves to travel, simply ask, "What kind of vacation would you be able to afford if you saved six hundred dollars on this purchase?" Helping customers to connect the value of the purchase to other substantial financial goals aids your customers in realizing that they are creating a path to achieving that goal. Price is not something you should fear; in reality, it is the much-needed assurance that helps customers understand that the buying decision is worth making.

Propose

The moment that most relationships see as the climax of their dating relationship is when the man decides to propose. It is the total of all his efforts micro focused into one moment. He may think back over their entire journey together as he contemplates how he wants to propose. He may want to incorporate some of her favorite things in the proposal, like her favorite candy, flowers, or song to make it personal and close the deal. No matter what route he takes, how big or small the plans are, or even the size of the ring.

A proposal becomes a proposal only after the man proposes. The act of asking the famous question, "Will you marry me?" is the most important moment of the entire effort and, for most people, the goal of the relationship. In most cases, the woman does not hesitate to answer because she already wanted to get married but could not say yes without someone asking the question.

Closing a sale works similarly. We cannot rely on the fact that we made an excellent introduction and presentation and were able to share the value of our product with our customers. We must be proactive when it is time to ask for the sale. Waiting for the customer to answer a pending question is leaving the work invested to chance. Just like a proposal, you must be proactive to close the sale and understand that not every customer will close the same way. The type of customer you are working with will determine the best closing technique to use.

Referrals

People love to refer their favorite things to others—favorite restaurant, movie, or book. When you build rapport, customers are excited to refer their friends and family to you, even if you do not ask. I once had a police officer who referred me to four of his fellow officers. Each time I sat down with one of them to write up the sale, I was told that I was the talk of the precinct. People whom I had not met wanted to do business with me because I built rapport.

Fulfillment

One of the greatest rewards of building rapport is the feeling of achievement that you receive from serving others. The stories that I heard and the moments of laughter that I shared with customers are what made my day special! There were days where I knew that I would bring the only smile they would have that day. This knowledge kept my day fun, exciting, and stress-free. Building rapport will help you to find purpose in your work.

The process of finding purpose in the work you do goes back to perspective. This objective is why forming proper perspective is the first step of the heart of sales. Until you see the impact you can to have on a customer's life as well as your own, you cannot feel fulfilled. Fulfillment aids in making the challenges meaningful, the difficulties purposeful, and the success transformational. Find the lessons in every situation, and decide to let them change you for the better.

The Heart of Sales is all about relationships. Relationships can be confusing, difficult, and even seem chaotic at times, but without relationships, we would not exist. The people we encounter during our life-span can influence us in ways we would never imagine, and the same is true about our opportunity to influence others. Although a career in sales has the potential to change our financial situation dramatically, we must remember that we are successful when we serve the customer. Serve first, sell second! Once you discover the hidden power that is a relationship where both parties benefit, you will find the very heartbeat of sales.

Conclusion

So did you hear it? Did you hear sales crying out to you in this book through the poetic depiction before each chapter? What may have sounded like a complicated relationship between two people, was an encounter many of us have had with sales. What appeared to be a date with twists and turns was the fear of the unknown that most people feel when interviewing for a sales job. Just like a relationship, the need for a sense of security can prevent us from venturing into the uncertainty of the dating world. That same need for security will stop us from stepping into the possibilities that are residing in sales.

Sales can feel uncertain because of the risk involved, but that risk opens us up to new opportunities and new realities. It gives us the chance to grow as professionals, helping us to develop our natural ability to connect with others and reach our individual goals. Both parties in the relationship should feel like they are offering something to the other and receiving from the other. Customers provide the opportunity to earn their trust and their business, while salespeople offer their product and their hearts to serve the customer. Both receive value from the exchange.

Regardless of your salary structure, there is one primary factor that determines your success, You! Sales is simply saying, "Believe in yourself, and you will believe in me." Dreams can become a stunning reality because you are the creator of that reality. When you focus on the potential rather than the challenges, your entire world can change through sales. Not only will your ability to communicate effectively with others drastically improve, but your capability to influence life to deliver your heart's desires will also become more powerful.

R. Deon Butler and I met during an interview for a 100 percent commission door-to-door sales opportunity in Atlanta, Georgia. He had no idea when he came to that interview that I would be taking him into a residential area to knock on doors, but once he found out, he was not excited. I was confident that he would not come back the next day, and when he left that interview, he was uncertain about the opportunity.

A simple step of faith on both our parts turned into the most impactful developmental season of our careers and a lifelong journey of genuine friendship, a committed friendship, resulting in what we are today as professionals and adults. In 2017, we incorporated Impact U Consulting, allowing us to share the gift of our knowledge in sales with leaders, professionals, and business owners. We know what sales has done for our lives, and we aim to help others thrive in their journey to success. Sales is the vehicle that can take any business to new heights, but to learn the art of sales, you must first be brave enough to pursue the heart of sales.

By now you must remember my high-school crush who moved away and left the teenage J. D. in shambles. We lost contact for a really long time, and both went about our lives. We got in touch some years down the line but only remained friends from a distance. Until one day, eighteen years after the first time I approached her in front of our high school, I felt the same spirit of boldness hit my soul. I reached out to her and relived that moment of walking across the school yard to talk to my crush.

Sales has taught me to never stop believing and to be bold enough to go after what you want in life. That young girl who handed me my first rejection is now the lady in my life. As we embark on our journey of love together, I can only be thankful that I did not allow fear to stop me those many years ago. You may have experienced heartbreak in your romantic relationships or failure in your professional life, but I am a witness that if you commit to never stop learning, you can have a *Happily Ever After.*

The End

Bibliography
The Holy Bible, NLT 2017

About the Author

Jean David Auguste and his business partner, R. Deon Butler, are the founders of Impact U Consulting, LLC, an organization focused on providing training products and solutions to improve employee productivity. A gifted motivational speaker and talent and development professional who specializes in teaching sales success, J. D. Auguste has passionate style of delivery, real-world experience, creative approach to training, and leadership skills that allow him to effectively equip his colleagues.

It's one thing to know sales; it's another thing to teach sales and live sales. His motivation is to empower professionals, entrepreneurs, and small-business owners by creating quality training products for the public.

Using lessons learned from his eighteen years of sales experience and rising to becoming a premier corporate trainer at multiple companies, J. D. Auguste now speaks, instructs, host seminars and facilitates highly impactful trainings nationwide for Impact U Consulting.

Please visit **ExperienceImpactU.com** for information on training courses currently being offered. Or **JDAuguste.com** to book J.D. as a speaker for your next event.

R. Deon Butler is a highly skilled communicator whose passion for Learning and Development has led to numerous achievements both Personally and Professionally. His unique ability to captivate his audience with humor and a down to earth style while yet motivating has allowed him to achieve numerous awards and recognition. In his 9 year tenure with Fortune 50 Top Company "Comcast", R. Deon Butler has earned multiple Top Sales Supervisor honors. After transitioning to a career in Adult Learning with Comcast University, R. Deon Butler would soon position himself as one of the most highly sought-after Sales Instructors in the entire company, earning the prestigious designation as Sr. Learning and Development Professional.

With over 20 years of experience, R. Deon Butler has earned a reputation as a "Sales Guru". His expertise includes, but not limited to Instructor-led training and virtual delivery. R. Deon Butler has an extensive catalog of content that he has trained: inbound/outbound sales, retention, face to face sales, leadership training, Train the Trainer and wireless sales to name a few. R. Deon Butler's philosophy is all about the experience the learner receives. He states," You may not remember everything that I taught you, but I guarantee you will remember the Experience."

Impact U Consulting LLC. Since 2017
ExperienceImpactU.com

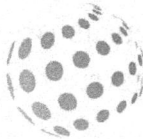

IMPACT
CONS**U**LTING